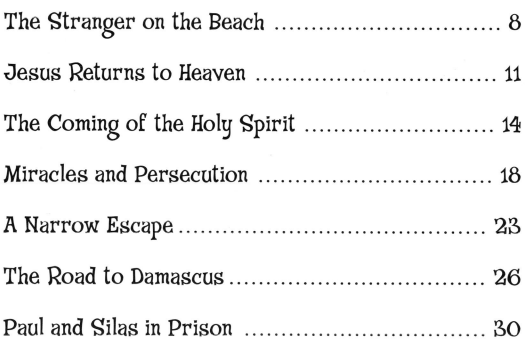

Contents

 Jesus and Doubting Thomas 4

 The Stranger on the Beach 8

Jesus Returns to Heaven 11

The Coming of the Holy Spirit 14

Miracles and Persecution 18

A Narrow Escape 23

The Road to Damascus 26

 Paul and Silas in Prison 30

 Paul at Sea 35

John's Vision of Heaven 38

Jesus and Doubting Thomas

Late morning on the third day after Jesus' death, Mary Magdalene burst into the room where the grieving disciples sat together. "I have seen Jesus!" she cried, flushed with excitement, and told them everything that had happened at the tomb. But as much as the disciples wanted to believe her, they couldn't.

Jesus Returns to Heaven

and other Bible Stories

Retold by Vic Parker

Miles Kelly

First published in 2011 by Miles Kelly Publishing Ltd
Harding's Barn, Bardfield End Green, Thaxted, Essex, CM6 3PX, UK

2 4 6 8 10 9 7 5 3 1

EDITORIAL DIRECTOR *Belinda Gallagher*
ART DIRECTOR *Jo Cowan*
EDITOR *Carly Blake*
DESIGNERS *Michelle Cannatella, Joe Jones*
JUNIOR DESIGNER *Kayleigh Allen*
COVER DESIGNER *Joe Jones*
CONSULTANT *Janet Dyson*
PRODUCTION MANAGER *Elizabeth Collins*
REPROGRAPHICS *Stephan Davis, Ian Paulyn*

ISBN 978-1-84810-403-7

Printed in China

British Library Cataloguing-in-Publication Data
A catalogue record for this book is available from the British Library

ACKNOWLEDGEMENTS
The publishers would like to thank the following artists
who have contributed to this book:

The Bright Agency Katriona Chapman, Dan Crisp,
Giuliano Ferri (inc. cover), Mélanie Florian

Advocate Art Andy Catling, Alida Massari

*The publishers would like to thank Robert Willoughby and
the London School of Theology for their help in compiling this book.*

Made with paper from a sustainable forest

www.mileskelly.net   info@mileskelly.net

www.factsforprojects.com

Self-publish your
children's book

buddingpress.co.uk

Meanwhile, two of Jesus' disciples were on their way from Jerusalem to the nearby village of Emmaus. As they walked with heavy hearts, a stranger joined them and began talking. To the disciples' astonishment, the stranger didn't seem to have heard anything of the events everyone was talking about – the death of Jesus and the disappearance of His body. However, he seemed to know the ancient holy writings very well and began explaining them.

"Don't you know that the holy men of old said that the Messiah would have to suffer to win glory?"

Later on the disciples shared a meal with the stranger and he blessed some bread, broke it into pieces and gave it to them. It was only then that they realized who he really was. "Jesus!" they gasped in astonishment. And at that moment, He disappeared.

The disciples hurried back to the city and went straight to tell the others – only to find that Jesus had appeared to Peter too!

Everyone began talking at once, full of excitement and asking to hear the stories again and again. No one noticed the newcomer arrive in their midst.

"Peace be with you," said Jesus, as everyone stood back in fear as though He was a ghost. "Don't be frightened," He said, "it's me. Look – here are the wounds on my hands and feet."

But one disciple was missing – Thomas. When his friends told Thomas what had happened he didn't believe it. Eight days later everyone was gathered again to talk and pray. Halfway through the meeting, Jesus appeared once more. "See for yourself, Thomas," He said. "Come and touch my wounds. Have faith – it's true."

Thomas broke down. "My Lord, it's really you," he sobbed.

"Bless you for believing," Jesus said gently. "But even more blessed are those who won't see me and yet will still believe."

Matthew chapter 28; Mark chapter 16;
Luke chapter 24; John chapter 20

The Stranger on the Beach

One evening, some of the disciples gathered at the Sea of Galilee. Peter wanted to take a little boat out and go fishing, just as he used to do in the days when he was a fisherman. Soon he and his friends, including James, John, Thomas and Nathaniel, were sailing out into open waters under a starry sky. How free and peaceful it felt – a welcome relief from the terrible events in the city in recent weeks.

All night, the disciples waited for fish to fill their nets, but when dawn came, their nets were all empty.

Then a voice floated across the waves. "Have you caught anything?"

Peering into the distance, the disciples could see the figure of a man on the shore.

"No, nothing." they yelled back.

"Try dropping your nets to the right side of the boat," came the voice.

The disciples thought it was worth a try. They soon felt their nets become heavy and they could hardly lift them.

Peter, James and John looked at each other and they remembered a time in the past when exactly the same thing had happened. "It's Jesus!" they exclaimed.

Peter couldn't wait to finish hauling in the catch and sail to shore, so he dived straight into the water and swam to be the first to reach Jesus.

Before long, Peter and the rest of the friends joined Jesus on the shore, and gathered around a little fire on the beach. They sat roasting fish for breakfast, and it was just like old times.

John chapter 21

Jesus Returns to Heaven

It was finally time for Jesus to leave the world for good. He gathered his disciples together and walked to the Mount of Olives, a short way from Jerusalem.

"Stay in the city for a while," Jesus told His eleven old friends. "You have already all been baptized once – by John the Baptist, with water. But soon you will all be baptized again – this time with the Holy Spirit. God is going to send you powerful gifts and I want you to use them by going out into the world and telling people in every country about me. Baptize all those who believe in me as my followers, in the name of the Father, the Son and the Holy Spirit. Teach them everything that I have taught you."

Jesus looked at His friends' worried faces. "Don't forget," He said gently, "I will be with you always, until the end of time."

With that, Jesus rose up into the air, higher and higher, until He disappeared into a blazing cloud of glory.

As the disciples squinted up at the dazzling light, it glimmered, gleamed and then faded… Jesus was gone but they carried on gazing up at the empty blue sky.

"Men of Galilee, what are you looking at?" came a voice. The disciples turned to find two men in glowing robes standing next to them.

"Jesus has gone, but one day He will come back to you in the same way."

Full of wonder and sadness, the disciples were comforted and made their way back to Jerusalem. They knew they would not see Jesus again soon, but were sure that one day He would return in glory.

Matthew chapter 28; Mark chapter 16; Luke chapter 24; Acts chapter 1

The Coming of the Holy Spirit

The disciples were in Jerusalem waiting for the Holy Spirit to somehow come and baptize them, as Jesus had told them.

Meanwhile they decided to replace the traitor, Judas Iscariot, with a new disciple. Then they would be twelve once more, as Jesus had originally intended. They prayed long and hard for guidance and cast votes, and finally Matthias was chosen. The twelve became known as the apostles. Then the waiting continued.

Fifty days after Passover and the death of Jesus, it was the feast of Pentecost – when Jews celebrated how God had given their religious laws to Moses.

The apostles were together, celebrating the feast, when suddenly a mighty sound like a rushing wind filled their ears as though it was all around them in the house. The apostles felt alive and full of energy, and turning to each other in astonishment, they saw that every man had a tiny flame hovering over his head.

"It must be the Holy Spirit!" they cried, and they found they were all speaking in different languages.

Realizing they had been blessed with the special gifts Jesus has talked about, the apostles excitedly ran out into the streets. Some found themselves giving thanks to God in Greek. Others were preaching about Jesus in Latin. Some were praising the Holy Spirit in Arabic, and many other languages.

Many worshippers from foreign lands had come to Jerusalem for Pentecost and they were stunned. "These men are from Galilee!" they marvelled. "How can they speak our language?"

However, some people just laughed and said that the apostles were drunk.

Then Peter began preaching and everyone who heard him was stirred by his passion. "We are not drunk," he laughed. "We are followers of Jesus of Nazareth. He has risen from the dead, we have seen it with our own eyes. Today we have been blessed by the Holy Spirit with these gifts of languages. Anyone who is truly sorry for their sins and follows the teachings of Jesus will be blessed too. Who wants to join us?"

That day the apostles baptized over three thousand people as followers of Jesus. The foundations of the Christian Church had been laid.

Acts chapters 1, 2

Miracles and Persecution

Every day after Pentecost, the apostles preached and worked miracles. And each day, more people were baptized as followers of Jesus.

One day, Peter and John were on their way into the temple to pray when they were stopped by a crippled beggar, asking for a few coins. "We have no money," Peter explained, "but what we do have I will give you… In the name of Jesus, get up and walk!" Peter reached out for the beggar's hand and encouraged him to get to his feet. The ragged man stood up and took a few unsteady paces. Then he began to dance with joy – and he danced all the way into the temple behind Peter and John.

The many worshippers there were utterly amazed. So Peter began speaking aloud, telling everyone about Jesus, how He had risen from the dead and about their God-given gifts of healing. Suddenly, some Jewish officials appeared. They were furious that the name of Jesus was once more causing a commotion among everyone in the temple. They had Peter and John thrown into prison for two days. But the men had committed no crime so they were freed.

Like all of the apostles, Peter did many astounding things in Jesus' name. He seemed to know things that he couldn't possibly know – unless God Himself had told him. He also performed many other great miracles of healing.

Sick people came from all over the country to sit in the streets of Jerusalem just in case Peter passed by. They believed that even if his shadow fell upon them, they would be cured. Of course, this enraged the Jewish officials further. Jesus was dead, but His name was still stirring up the people so the Jewish officials put Peter and John in prison once more. However that very night they found that the two men had vanished! Upon finding the two apostles teaching in the temple, the Jewish officials' explanation was that an angel had come and released them. The confused, furious officials then had Peter and John beaten, and ordered them never to speak the name of Jesus again.

Of course, this didn't stop the apostles. Every day, the number of followers of Jesus grew. The time came when the Jewish officials finally decided that enough was enough and they accused one apostle, Stephen, of blasphemy and stoned him to death. He was the first man ever to die in the name of Jesus. Next they sent soldiers to every house in Jerusalem, and then through the rest of Judea too, searching for other followers to arrest. Little did the officials know they were part of God's great plan.

The apostles fled to safety to lands far and wide, taking the word of Jesus to many thousands of people who wouldn't otherwise have heard it.

Acts chapters 2, 4, 5, 7, 8

A Narrow Escape

As he travelled around, Peter worked many miracles in the name of Jesus. In a town called Lydda, in north-east Judea, he healed a paralyzed man. In the town of Joppa, he brought Tabitha, a woman who had died, back to life. Only Jesus Himself and the great prophets Elijah and Elisha had ever been granted this gift. Peter preached to Jews and non Jews alike, because he knew that everyone was equal in the eyes of God. He also baptized the first non Jews to follow Jesus.

Meanwhile, King Herod Agrippa became just as determined as the Jewish officials to get rid of the 'trouble-making' Christians. He was a wicked man and he had James, the brother of John, put to death. Then he had Peter the leader of the apostles arrested and put on trial. Flung into a dungeon, Peter was chained to two soldiers, with a round-the-clock guard outside his door. Herod heard how Peter and John had escaped from prison before, and was taking no chances.

But the night before Peter was to be tried, he dreamt that a light blazed into his

cell and an angel woke him. "Get up quickly!" the angel commanded. Peter felt his chains fall away, realizing that it wasn't a dream. Then he followed the angel past the guards and out into the street.

The next day, when Herod heard of Peter's escape, he sent soldiers out after him. But Peter was nowhere to be found.

Acts chapters 9, 10, 12

The Road to Damascus

One of the Jewish officers who was determined to wipe out Christians was a young man called Saul. He became famous and feared as a ruthless persecutor of the followers of Jesus.

Saul had been brought up as a Pharisee – a very strict Jew – and he felt that Jesus' apostles were undoing all the ancient laws he held to be important. Saul had decided to seek out Christians – not just in Jerusalem, or even Judea, but in other countries too. He went to the high priest in Jerusalem and asked for letters of introduction to the synagogues in Damascus, the capital of Syria, so he could find and arrest followers of Jesus there.

Soon Saul was on his way. As the great city loomed before him, a flash of lightning blazed from the sky and struck him off his horse. Saul grovelled in the dirt, shaken to the core. Somehow he knew it hadn't been an accident.

"Saul, Saul, why are you persecuting me?" a voice boomed into his mind.

"Who – who are you?" the terrified Saul managed to stutter, shutting his eyes against the dazzle.

"I am Jesus, whom you have sworn to persecute," the voice roared. "Now get up, go into the city and wait there."

The voice was gone, the light faded and Saul opened his eyes.

Everything was black… He was blind!

The soldiers accompanying Saul were puzzled. They led him into the city and found a place for him to stay. There Saul sat for two days, refusing to talk to anyone or even eat or drink.

On the third day, there was a knock at the door. Saul's soldiers opened it to an old man named Ananias. "God has sent me to you," Ananias explained. "He told me that He has chosen you to spread His message – not just to the Jews, but to non Jews too."

Gently, Ananias laid his hands on Saul's head and the darkness gradually became light, as if scales fell from his eyes, and he could see again.

Overwhelmed with relief and joy, Saul fell to his knees and gave thanks to God. Then he asked Ananias to baptize him!

When Saul had recovered from his ordeal, he went straight to the synagogues of Damascus as he had planned. But instead of arresting Christians, he preached that Jesus was the Son of God.

Acts chapters 8, 9

Paul and Silas in Prison

At first, people found it difficult to believe that Saul had gone from being a sworn enemy of Jesus to one of His most passionate followers. To give people an outward sign of his change of heart, Saul changed his name to Paul.

He managed to win trust by putting even more energy and effort into finding new followers for Jesus. As a Pharisee, Paul had great knowledge of the ancient sacred writings, and could argue in support of Jesus with the Jewish officials in Jerusalem too. How they came to hate their former favourite, Saul! Eventually the apostles discovered that the officials were plotting to kill Paul, so they sent him far to the north to the city of Tarsus, where he could preach out of danger.

That was the beginning of many years of travelling for Paul, teaching the messages of Jesus to people all around the Mediterranean. Often accompanied by other apostles, such as Barnabas and John, he made one journey after another. He taught non Jews about God, from Syria to Cyprus, and Turkey to Greece, and baptized thousands in the name of Jesus.

However Paul and his friends faced many dangers. Angry Jews hated them for baptizing non Jews, and non Jews hated them for saying that the idols they worshipped were false. Even when Paul and his companions were chased out of town, or suffered violence, they weren't put off. In fact they became even more determined. Every single soul they won for God gave them great joy.

Paul and his fellow apostle Silas were once in Macedonia when they were accused of 'disturbing the peace', and were whipped and thrown into prison. However they refused to be downhearted. They began singing hymns to God, and the other prisoners joined in too.

At midnight, the sudden sound of
rumbling drowned out the apostles' voices.
The prison walls shook and started to
crumble. The terrified prisoners were thrown

from side to side. Their chains broke and
their cell doors burst open.

All the prisoners could have seized the
opportunity to escape, but Paul and Silas

talked everyone into staying put. When the jailer ran in with his guards, he couldn't believe it. He had been ready to take his own life if all of the prisoners had run away while under his responsibility. The jailer ordered for them to be chained up again, all except for Paul and Silas who were taken to his house. There, the jailer fell on his knees before them and asked them to tell him more about Jesus.

By the time dawn came, the jailer and his whole household had been baptized.

Acts chapters 10, 11, 13 to 16

Paul at Sea

Paul became well known for having mysterious powers and working great miracles of healing. He once brought a boy called Eutychus back to life, who had died by falling out of a window.

Before returning to Jerusalem one year for the feast of Pentecost, the Holy Spirit warned him that imprisonment and suffering lay ahead. Paul was not scared. He was ready to die for Jesus if he needed to.

In Jerusalem the Jewish officials had Paul arrested for supposedly breaking holy rules. They accused him of encouraging Jewish Christians to ignore the ancient laws of Moses. They also accused him of sneaking non Jews into the sacred temple – all untrue charges. Paul found himself in prison yet again, with enemies who wanted him dead.

Eventually, he was freed, but he was placed under house arrest and unable to go anywhere for two years. Finally Paul had enough. He had been born in Rome and as a Roman citizen he claimed his right to be tried by the emperor himself.

Paul set sail for Rome, but on the voyage his ship ran into a raging storm. In a dream an angle told him the ship would sink but everyone would survive. And so it happened. The ship was tossed onto a sandbank and battered by waves. All of the people onboard were washed up alive on the island of Malta.

On finally reaching Rome, Paul was put under house arrest again, for a further two years. So he spent his time writing letters to friends, urging them to live good lives and trust in God.

And that's how Paul lived until he was finally put to death.

Acts chapters 17 to 28

John's Vision of Heaven

The apostle John was praying one day, when he heard a voice say, "Write down what I am going to show you and send it to the followers of Jesus."

John span around, and there was Jesus, shining with light. John fell at His feet but Jesus said gently, "Don't be afraid. I am the first and the last. I am the Living One who was dead. Now I shall live forever. Watch – I will show you the future."

John saw a vision of a door opening into Heaven, revealing God surrounded by singing angels.

He was shown marvel after marvel. The battle between good and evil playing out on the Earth, and the end of the world when Jesus was triumphant, hurling the devil into a lake of fire. John saw God passing judgement on all who had ever lived. If a person's name was not in the Lord's great book, they were destroyed with their master, Satan.

Then John was shown a new Heaven and Earth, and out of Heaven came a vision of a new Jerusalem. The city gleamed and glittered as though it was made from gold and jewels of many rainbow colours. Through the city flowed the River of Life, its water as clear as crystal. God Himself was living there. His Kingdom on Earth had come.

John heard Jesus speaking one last time. "I will be coming soon, and I shall reward the good with blessings forever."

And John whispered, "Amen!"

Revelation chapters 1, 4, 5, 19 to 22